Balance

A guide to life's forgotten pleasures

How to *give a foot massage.*

fig 1.
Find someone with feet.

fig 2.
Rub firmly, deliberately pushing
outwardly with thumbs.
(No tickling.)

fig 3.
Beg recipient to return favor.

How to *turn your hand into a plane.*

fig 1.
Roll down car window.

fig 2.
Push arm into oncoming wind.

fig 3.
Playfully dip hand up and down.
Make jet noises with mouth.

How to *make a tree swing.*

fig 1.

Needed: Large, friendly tree.
Rope. Board with hole.

fig 2.

Tie big honkin' knots around
limb and under board.

fig 3.

Swing. Spin. Swing.
(Thank tree when finished.)

How to *make a blanket fort.*

fig 1.
Get largest blanket
you can find.

fig 2.
Drape blanket across backs
of chairs, or other furniture.

fig 3.
Occupy fort. Consume snacks.

How to *call in well.*

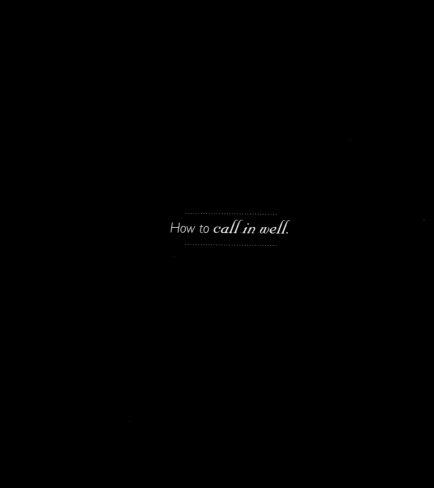

fig 1.
Call boss.

fig 2.
Explain that you feel
wonderful, and will be in
"first-thing" tomorrow.

fig 3.
Ever so gently, hang up.

skip stones.

fig 1.

In a nutshell: Rocks with edges,
bad. Rocks without edges, good.

fig 2.

Bring arm back slowly. Stay low.
Attempt to keep stone parallel
with water's surface.

fig 3.

Let 'er rip. Count number of skips.
(Note: One "kerplunk" does not
count as a skip.)

How to *look for shooting stars.*

fig 1.
Wait for night.
(After midnight is best.)

fig 2.
Go outside. Find comfy spot.
Recline.

fig 3.
Gaze into heavens. Prepare to be
awestruck by wonders of nature.

How to *make noise with a blade of grass.*

fig 1.

Find a nice, flat piece of grass.

fig 2.

Place between thumbs.
Clasp hands.

fig 3.

Blow until you get a sound.
Note: Sounds will not be as
pretty as depicted here.

How to *unplug the phone.*

fig 1.

Assess whether ringing in
ears is real or imaginary.

fig 2.

Resist strong desire
to rip cord from wall.

fig 3.

Gently remove plug.
(Make lemonade.)

How to *do a logroll*.

fig 1.
Survey hill for rocks.

fig 2.
Think like a log.
Roll baby, roll.

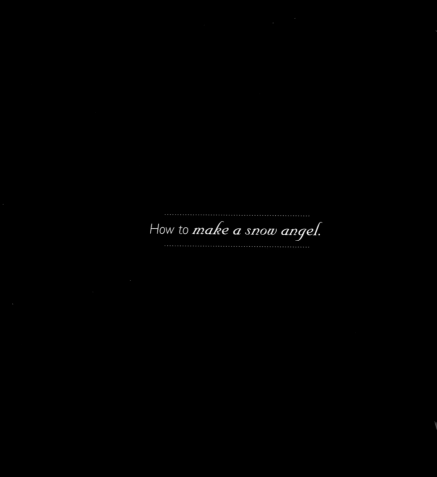

How to *make a snow angel.*

fig 1.
Lie down in fresh snow.

fig 2.
Flap arms and spread
legs a few times.

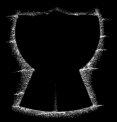

fig 3.
Get up. Evaluate angel.
Make more.

How to *have chicken fights*.

fig 1.

Divide (diplomatically) into pairs.

fig 2.

Climb aboard partner's shoulders.

fig 3.

Thrash about like chickens
(until realizing how utterly
ridiculous you all look).

....
How to *sleep in*.
....

fig 1.

Strange buzzing sound
interrupts flying dream.

fig 2.

Beat innocent "clock"
into submission.

fig 3.

Resume flight.

How to *catch a snowflake on your tongue.*

fig 1.
Go outside against
better judgment.

fig 2.
Stick tongue out.

fig 3.
Carefully align tongue with
falling drop/flake. (Repeat.)

How to *blow bubbles*.

fig 1.
Chew gum until
nice & stretchy.

fig 2.
Insert tongue into
gum and remove.

fig 3.
Blow gently, yet confidently.
Wait for explosion.

How to *watch clouds*.

fig 1.
Go outside.

fig 2.
Recline. Look up.

fig 3.
Watch as clouds become
fire engines, poodles, shoes,
old friends, etc.

How to *make someone's day*.

fig 1.
Find stressed-out associate.

fig 2.
Pass by casually.
Offer compliment. "Great haircut."
Or, "Wow, cool dress."

fig 3.
Watch from afar as associate
is magically revived.

How to *listen*.

fig 1.

Notice you are doing
most of the talking.

fig 2.

Shut mouth.

fig 3.

Open seldom-used holes
in side of head.

How to *fly a kite.*

fig 1.

Have friend/stranger
hold kite. Unwind string.

fig 2.

Allow friend/stranger to let go
when they "feel the moment."

fig 3.

Do not hog kite.

How to *make a shadow puppet.*

fig 1.
Turn off all big, overhead lights.

fig 2.
Shine light onto wall or
ceiling. Contort hand weirdly
and place into light.

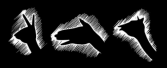

fig 3.
Rabbit. Dog. Ostrich? (Llama??)

How to *write a letter.*

fig 1.

Accept cold fact that you never get
letters because you never send any.

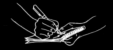

fig 2.

Write friends or loved ones. Say
mushy things you would never
say face to face.

fig 3.

Hand-drop letter in box. (Check
door twice, even though they never
get stuck.) Wait for reply.

How to *look for a four-leaf clover.*

fig 1.

Find meadow (or unkept lawn).

fig 2.

Get down on all fours.
Begin meticulous search.

fig 3.

Examine prize closely
(beware of impostors). Wait for
good luck to take effect.

How to *hug*.

fig 1.
Seek out melancholy
friend.

fig 2.
Open arms wide.
Approach boldly.

fig 3.
Wrap arms around victim.
Squeeze for 8-15 seconds.

How to *tickle*.

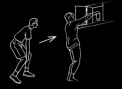

fig 1.

Wait for maximum
vulnerability.

fig 2.

Go in for the kill.

fig 3.

Scram.

How to *go barefoot.*

fig 1.

Listen for tiny screams
emanating from feet.

fig 2.

Remove shoes and socks.

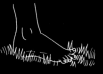

fig 3.

Walk around in grass (or sand).
Wiggle toes often.

How to *pretend you can fly*.

fig 1.
Find a good spot for take-off.

fig 2.
Close eyes. Think bird thoughts.

fig 3.
Spread arms. Fly.

How to *take a nap.*

fig 1.

Search for perfect tree.

fig 2.

Find snuggliest part
of trunk for pillow.

fig 3.

Snooze.

How to *take a different way home.*

fig 1.

When leaving work, assess damage
done to soul from daily commute.

fig 2.

Fight temptation to
embrace the familiar.

fig 3.

Go different way. Navigate home
relying heavily on faith and luck.

How to *do a somersault.*

fig 1.

Make sure ground is forgiving.

fig 2.

Tuck in head. Thrust body
forward. Go with flow.

fig 3.

Stay calm until help arrives.

How to *turn off the TV* .

fig 1.

Notice that mind and body
are numb.

fig 2.

Hit same button you used
to turn TV "on."

fig 3.

Walk out nearest opening.

How to *be neighborly.*

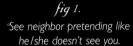

fig 1.
"See neighbor pretending like
he/she doesn't see you.

fig 2.
Raise arm and wave vigorously
while simultaneously bellowing,
"Howdy, neighbor!"

fig 3.
Magically, neighbor responds.
(Works every time, guaranteed.)

How to *have a picnic.*

fig 1.
Collect assorted goodies.

fig 2.
Find secluded spot. (Living room
will suffice in a pinch.)

fig 3.
Chat. Eat. Look around.
Eat. Chat. Eat more.

How to *do a cartwheel.*

fig 1.

*If you can't even do this, please
do not read any further.*

fig 2.

*Bend over. Place hands
flat on ground. Thrust legs
over, one at a time.*

fig 3.

*Continue until other leg contacts
ground. Stand upright. (Wait for
imaginary standing ovation.)*

How to *open doors for strangers.*

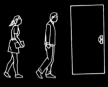

fig 1.

Approach door as you
normally would.

fig 2.

Open door. Fight blinding urge
to be first at everything. Allow
stranger to pass ahead of you.

fig 3.

Reflect briefly on the
power of simple acts.

How to *make s'mores.*

fig 1.

Hold marshmallows over fire.
Remove only when <u>you</u>
believe they are done.
(Beware of s'mores "experts.")

fig 2.

Swiftly slide marshmallows off
stick onto chocolate bar and
encase with graham crackers.

fig 3.

Consume immediately. Open
discussion on society's obsession
with fat-free foods.

How to *skinny-dip*.

fig 1.

Find secluded spot.

fig 2.

Remove all remnants of civilization.

fig 3.

Dive in. Acclimate to nakedness.
(Relax, this can take a while.)

How to *follow a bug around.*

fig 1.
Find nomadic bug.

fig 2.
Get down to bug's level.

fig 3.
Go anywhere bug goes.
(Except to work.)

How to *give a piggyback ride.*

fig 1.

Convince friend to abandon
pride and hop onto your back.

fig 2.

Have friend hold on to shoulders —
not hair, head, or ears.

fig 3.

Run around. Listen closely
for unabashed giggling.

How to *answer the phone differently.*

fig 1.

Hear phone ring for
umpteenth time.

fig 2.

Pick up receiver as you
normally would.

fig 3.

Instead of saying "hello?" boldly
answer, "Ruby's Pig-shack!" or
"What time you got?"

How to *be spontaneous.*

fig 1.
Ponder canceling
appointments.

fig 2.
Cancel appointments.

fig 3.
Make beeline to nearest
swimming hole.

How to *give a noogie*.

fig 1.
Sneak up behind
friend or loved one.

fig 2.
Secure head beneath chin.

fig 3.
Rub knuckles back and forth on
victim's head. (Note: Not a good
idea on folks in bad moods.)

How to *fish*.

fig 1.
Eagerly cast line
into water.

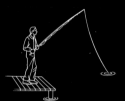

fig 2.
Wait.

fig 3.
Wait more.

How to *make a wish.*

fig 1.
Find weed puffball.
Yank.

fig 2.
Look up. Make a wish.

fig 3.
Blow. Wait a while.
(Wish should eventually
come true.)

How to *make a water balloon.*

fig 1.
Purchase balloons
at favorite retailer.

fig 2.
Fill balloon with water.
(Do not overfill.)

fig 3.
Seek enemy.

How to *do an underwater handstand.*

fig 1.
Find body of water.

fig 2.
Take big ol' deep breath
and head to bottom.

fig 3.
Push up until legs poke out. Hold.
Note: It usually feels like legs were
straighter than they actually were.